D1784389

Original title:
The Poppy Perspective

Author: Oliver Bennett
ISBN HARDBACK: 978-1-80566-697-4
ISBN PAPERBACK: 978-1-80566-982-1

A Canvas of Remembrance

In fields where colors dance with glee,
A poppy's thought is quite carefree.
It mixes red with thoughts so bright,
And giggles daily, quite a sight!

With whispers soft, it quips with cheer,
"I bloom for joy, not for a tear!"
Old battles fade, but here I stand,
With petals light, an artist's hand!

Oh, who would think a flower bold,
Could share a joke much like the old?
A splash of laughter, a breeze so sweet,
In every blossom, humor's treat!

So paint your days with shades so bright,
Let memories linger in pure delight.
For every hue has tales to tell,
In laughter, where we weave quite well!

Fragile Voices of Summer

Whispers float on gentle air,
Summer's giggles everywhere.
Poppies tease the bumblebee,
"Hey there friend, come dance with me!"

They sway and bend, a silly show,
Tickling each leaf with a blow.
"What's that you say?" a voice in jest,
"I'm here to bloom and do my best!"

As sunbeams play their hide and seek,
The flowers chuckle, oh so sleek.
With fragile voices, sweet and free,
They sing of love and jubilee!

In fields where giggles float like mist,
Amid the blooms, you can't resist.
Join the laughter, sing along,
In summer's heart, we all belong!

Echoes from the Soil

Beneath the earth, a secret lay,
With tiny giggles, roots at play.
"Did you hear that?" one whispers low,
"A flower's dream begins to grow!"

Echoes dance from deep below,
A laughter shared, a gentle flow.
"We've seen the world, it's quite a spree!"
"Let's tickle blossoms, wild and free!"

As seedlings sprout, they boast and grin,
"Who knew that soil housed fun within?"
Jokes from the ground, a playful scheme,
In every bloom, a little dream!

When petals open, laughter shows,
Echoes rise where sunshine glows.
In every root, a story thrived,
With giggles soft, the earth contrived!

Blooming Beneath the Weight of Time

Time leans heavy on each bloom,
Yet laughter slices through the gloom.
"Oh time, you joke!" a poppy sighs,
"I bloom regardless; watch me rise!"

With every day, a dance ensues,
In evening light, a playful muse.
"Let's break the clock, let's twirl and spin,
For laughter lives where joys begin!"

Beneath the weight, a heart that's light,
Sees beauty blooming, day and night.
"Oh darling minutes, don't be shy!"
"With every petal, we reach the sky!"

So let the days flow wild and free,
In every petal, a memory.
For time can't hold a vibrant heart,
With every bloom, a brand new start!

The Art of a Fragile Dream

In a garden where giggles sprout,
A dream took flight with a silly shout.
Blossoms danced in a gentle breeze,
Tickling bees with the sweetest tease.

Petals wobbled like Jell-O at play,
While butterflies giggled, 'Is it a game today?'
Each sip of sun a playful joke,
As clouds joined in with a fluffy poke.

A daisy winked, a tulip sighed,
With whispers of fun, they'd not abide.
Over the hill, the laughter rang,
In the heart of the flower bed, joy sang.

So let's tiptoe in this fragile scheme,
And find the humor in every dream.
For life's too short for a frown or pout,
Join the dance; let your fun shine out.

Whimsical Paths of Wildflowers

There's a path where wild thoughts bloom bright,
With flowers giggling in morning light.
They frolic and play, no care in sight,
Tickling toes that wander by, oh what a sight!

Bumbles buzz with a cheeky cheer,
"Follow us, join the party, dear!"
A daisied dress invited, so gay,
Spinning laughter along the way.

A dandelion shouted, "Let's make a wish!"
While petals advised, "Oh, do it with a twist!"
They twisted and twirled in colors so bright,
Even the sun seemed to smile at their flight.

So take a turn on this whimsical spree,
Let wild laughter set your spirit free.
With every step, feel the joyful sway,
In the garden of giggles, forever stay!

Shadows of Silent Blooms

In the twilight, where shadows creep,
The blossoms chuckle, secrets to keep.
They whispered 'bout antics in full display,
As nightfall came to join the fray.

A rose leaned in with a cheeky grin,
"Shh, the daisies are plotting again!"
In whispers of petals all colors designed,
Each bloom crafted giggles, oh so divine.

They shivered and shimmered beneath the moon,
Casting laughter like a silvery tune.
A nightingale chimed in with a song,
Encouraging shadows to dance along.

So tiptoe softly where blooms doth hide,
In the laughter of petals, joy does reside.
For in the shadows of silent dreams,
Even flowers know how sweet fun seems!

Petal Promises and Raindrops

Petals promised a day of delight,
With raindrops falling, it felt just right.
"Let's skip the gloom and dance with glee!"
Laughed the flowers, happy as can be.

In puddles reflecting their colors so bold,
They splashed and played, never feeling cold.
A butterfly dipped for a funny prank,
While a shy bud blushed and quietly sank.

"Watch out for puddles, you're hopping too high!"
Cried a daffodil with a twinkling eye.
But the raindrops laughed as they bounced around,
Creating a symphony of joy profound.

So let's twirl under this drizzly embrace,
And savor the laughter in nature's grace.
For even in rain, promises bloom,
In the garden of joy, there's always room!

Blossoms in the Sunlight

In the garden, bugs take a break,
Sunshine hugs every petal's ache.
Bees wear shades, buzzing with flair,
While ants parade without a care.

Rabbits munch on salad greens,
Wearing hats made from magazine scenes.
Sunflowers grin, looking quite wise,
As daisies compete for sunlit skies.

A caterpillar shimmies and groans,
Dreaming of skies, far from his own.
Raggedy leaves burst into song,
Join us here, you can't be wrong!

Butterflies twirl like they're on stage,
While worms write the tales of the age.
With laughter spilled on the soft, warm ground,
In this wild world, joy's always found.

Dancing with the Wind's Embrace

Grass blades sway in a jolly romp,
Tickled by breeze, they jiggle and stomp.
Squirrels giggle, hiding their snacks,
As clouds drift by with playful hacks.

The trees are twirling, wearing green gowns,
While stray breezes play pranks on towns.
A kite takes flight, dancing with glee,
As birds join in with a sweet jubilee.

Chasing the shadows, we stumble and laugh,
While sunbeams tease with a cheeky staff.
In a world turned topsy-turvy with fun,
Every leaf whispers secrets, just begun.

At sunset, the colors swirl with delight,
Painting giggles that last through the night.
With each breeze that rustles our hair,
Life winks at us, and we're light as air.

Fields of Crimson Dreams

In fields so bright, where laughter blooms,
Every flower plots joyous cartoons.
Vermilion jokes hide 'tween the leaves,
Tickling toes, like playful thieves.

Bouncing butterflies, mischief in flight,
Tell tall tales of the best sunset bite.
While ladybugs play tag on the grass,
Hoping the wind will help them pass.

Crickets chirp with rhythmic delight,
As the sun melts down, bidding goodnight.
Every crumpled leaf joins the cheer,
For dreams are better when friends are near.

Stars peek out, their laughter a treat,
While nature dances on twinkling feet.
In these fields, we weave from day's thread,
With every giggle, our spirits are fed.

Tales Woven in Vermilion

In a tapestry made of wild red blooms,
Squirrels spin stories from sunny rooms.
The sun sneezes, and shadows can't stay,
As petals tell jokes in a bright bouquet.

Hummingbirds hum a melodious theft,
Swiping sweet nectar, feeling quite deft.
While daisies giggle, gossiping near,
About that rogue tulip, oh dear, oh dear!

Wind chimes laugh with a tinkling cheer,
As the moon peeks out, whispering near.
With every rustle, our hearts feel light,
In this garden of laughter, day turns to night.

So join the fun, let your worries fly,
In the bonkers world where flowers sigh.
As vermilion hugs the last fading light,
We giggle together, all wrong feels right.

The Courage to Blossom

In a garden so bright and bold,
Petals dance, stories unfold.
With laughter behind tiny seams,
They twirl in the sunlight's beams.

Bees buzzing with joyous cheer,
Tickle the blooms, never a fear.
Each bud laughs at the show,
As they wiggle and sway below.

Roots deep down, giggle and snicker,
While worms wiggle, oh how they bicker!
Every bloom has courage inside,
In the play of colors, they take pride.

So raise a glass to the flowers' fun,
For in every petal, a jest is spun.
With courage to blossom in tutti-frutti glee,
Life's a garden, let it be free!

Beneath the Velvet Sky

Underneath a sky so deep,
Flowers whisper secrets they keep.
Each sunset paints a silly face,
As daisies giggle in their embrace.

Night brings stars with a twinkling laugh,
While clovers plot a silly giraffe.
They challenge ferns to a dance-off,
And tease each other, 'Would you scoff?'

Moss hangs out in a cozy nook,
With butterflies, they share a book.
Each bloom beams with mischief's delight,
In a velvet sky, all feels just right.

Together they sway in moonlight's hum,
Making memories, the night's never done!
For beneath this dreamy, cushy plot,
Every giggle ties the garden knot.

Resplendent Souls in Chromatic Harmony

In hues that sparkle, flowers ignite,
An orchestra of colors, what a sight!
With laughter as loud as a trumpet's roar,
They join in harmony, wanting more.

The reds and yellows dance side by side,
While blues tell jokes that cause them to glide.
Each petal a note, each stem a chord,
Resplendent souls in laughter they hoard.

Purple laughs at expectations and norms,
In this garden, creativity warms.
With petals en pointe, they spin and twirl,
Silly blooms, the hearts of the world.

So join this garden rave, oh dear,
Where colors laugh, and jokes are sincere.
Together they shine, a radiant crew,
In this symphony of laughter, they grew!

The Language of Blooming Beauty

In fields of chatter, flowers convene,
Speaking in colors, lively and keen.
With petals like mouths, they giggle and tease,
Explaining their secrets with buzzing ease.

The daisies declare, 'Wear your best hat!'
While the roses just laugh, 'Look at that!'
A tulip adds, 'Let's throw a bash!'
All blooms join in, they break out in a splash.

Their language is a dance, fresh and spry,
Every sway a syllable, reaching for the sky.
In hues so vivid, spirits unite,
With humor, they bloom, pure and bright.

So listen closely, you'll hear them sing,
In the laughter of petals, joy takes wing.
For beauty is blooming and humor's the way,
In this flowery chatter, let's all play!

Unraveling Stories in the Meadow

In a field where tall grass sways,
The flowers giggle in sunlit rays.
A bee tried to dance, fell on his bum,
And whispered, "Oops! Did you see that, Mum?"

The butterflies flutter, wear silly hats,
Questioning why they are often chased by cats.
A ladybug lost, tried to hitch a ride,
But the worm said, "No way! I'm not that wide!"

A Journey through the Red Horizon.

Rolling hills, a sunset glow,
A picnic where unexpected guests do show.
A squirrel stole my sandwich with glee,
He stopped for a selfie, just to tease me!

A robin sang tunes, quite out of tune,
Announcing a party to start very soon.
The ants donned bowties, ready to dance,
While I wondered if I'd missed my chance!

Whispers of the Scarlet Bloom

Underneath the bright blue sky,
A blossom shouted, "You can't just fly!"
A bee buzzed back, "I beg to differ,
I'm making honey; now that's my quiver!"

A snail with shades said, "Life moves fast,
But I'm on my own time; I'll never be last!"
The daisies chuckled at the blooming frown,
Because even slowpokes can wear a crown!

Through the Eyes of a Red Petal.

In a garden where laughter brews,
Roses wear shoes, they dance in twos.
A clover jokes, "I'm lucky, indeed!",
As grasshoppers try to plant a seed.

The sunflowers point, "Look at you down there!
With your petal-twirled hair, how do you dare?"
A chubby bumblebee passed with a grunt,
And said, "Keep blooming, you quirky runt!"

Nature's Scarlet Dreams

In the meadow, bright and bold,
Dreams of red in tales unfold.
Bumblebees in silly dance,
Whisper secrets, take a chance.

Green grass giggles, sways with ease,
Tickled by the playful breeze.
Butterflies in polka dots,
Argue over sweet nectar spots.

Rabbits hop in jaunty style,
Sharing carrots with a smile.
Nature's mischief all around,
In every bloom, laughter found.

A Symphony of Fragile Moments

In the wind, a chirp, a trill,
Nature's orchestra, never still.
Caterpillars wearing hats,
Join the show, what funny cats!

Raindrops tap, a rhythmic treat,
Dancing puddles at our feet.
Squirrels sing with nutty flair,
While frogs croon in their wet lair.

A breeze makes all the petals sway,
As flowers giggle, come what may.
A song of joy, a funny rhyme,
In nature's play, we lose all time.

Cultivating Quiet Strength

In the soil, worms wiggle round,
Silent workers underground.
Seeds in rows, they make a fuss,
Rising up, no need to rush.

Sunflowers bend to see the sun,
In sunlit games, they all have fun.
Bees wear jackets, oh so grand,
Buzzing cheerfully, lending a hand.

Roots hold tight, a secret feat,
While weeds try to take a seat.
Strength in silence, plants prevail,
With laughter on a leafy trail.

When Colors Speak of Change

Red leaves twirl, a crisp ballet,
Chasing summer far away.
Pumpkins laugh in orange glow,
Wearing sweaters, nice and low.

Winter's chill begins to creep,
Frosty nights, the world's asleep.
Snowflakes dance, a sparkly spree,
Whispering secrets, just to me.

Springtime giggles, blooms arise,
Colors burst, to our surprise.
Nature's laughter fills the air,
In every shift, a playful dare.

Breath of the Whispering Flowers

In a garden bright, where petals sway,
Bees plot their dance, come what may.
Chasing blooms, they buzz around,
While butterflies wear crowns they found.

A tulip twirls in a breezy spin,
"Watch me whirl!" it says with a grin.
Dandelions cheer, blowing puffed seeds,
Launching wishes like tiny steeds.

Sunflowers giggle, so tall and proud,
As crows croak jokes that draw a crowd.
"Why so sunny?" they tease the day,
"Because laughter keeps the clouds at bay!"

With colors bright and spirits high,
Nature's jesters laugh and sigh.
In this floral realm, fun never ends,
As petals and chatter become fast friends.

A Daydream Among Yellow and Red

A butterfly dreams of chocolate cake,
While ladybugs plot their next mistake.
"Let's skip the rain!" they giggle and grin,
As they dance past tulips, under their skin.

The sun shines bright on a splash of hue,
While rabbits play cards, but they haven't a clue.
"Are we betting carrots?" one mischievous cries,
"Oh please, just let me nap," another replies!

In this riot of colors, a bust of delight,
The daisies caper, filled with sheer light.
While wind whispers secrets, oh so absurd,
As the roses just blush and can't say a word.

"Why are we here?" asks a bold violette,
"Who knows," laughs the marigold, "isn't it great?"
With petals unfurling, they giggle and sway,
Lost in the hilarity of the bright, sunny day.

Legacy of Crimson Whispers

In a field of whispers, where colors collide,
Crimson blooms gossip, side by side.
"Did you hear the news?" a poppy declares,
"Bee on the loose, causing quite stares!"

The daisies burst out in fits of glee,
"Tell us more, please! Oh, what could it be?"
A grasshopper hops like he owns the scene,
Hoping for laughs, feeling quite keen.

"Once I saw a snail with an enormous hat,
He looked so ridiculous, just like that!"
The flowers all chuckle, in hues bright and loud,
Cracking up together, oh what a crowd!

Crimson continues, "And let's not forget,
That dandelion who made quite a bet!"
With laughter echoing through the warm breeze,
Each tale they tell brings joy with such ease.

The Silence of Scarlet Elegy

In twilight's glow, the petals recline,
The roses, in whispers, their gossip divine.
"Where's that bee?" asks a curious bud,
"Probably stuck in the jam of a mud!"

An ivy vine chuckles with leafy delight,
"Maybe he's dancing with moths of the night!"
While nearby, a daffodil hums a sweet tune,
"Imagine if flowers could waltz under the moon!"

Scarlet blooms ponder, their laughter abounds,
In the garden of whispers, pure joy surrounds.
"What if we painted the sky purple instead?
Then no one could frown," the laughter is spread.

So style your petals, paint colors so bright,
In this silly symphony, laughter takes flight.
For even in silence, the blooms find their cheer,
In giggling soft petals, all gathered near.

Crimson Dreams in a Golden Field

In fields of gold beneath the sun,
A poppy dreams of all its fun.
It sways with grace, a silly dance,
In breezy winds, it takes a chance.

Oh, how it giggles, quite absurd,
Chatting with bugs, the cheeky bird.
"Why don't you join me?" it declares,
With petals bright, it doesn't care.

A busy bee, it buzzes by,
"Come on, old friend, don't be so shy!"
But bees are serious, on their quest,
While poppies jest and never rest.

The golden grains, they laugh away,
As poppies dance, lead the display.
In crimson dreams, they spin and twirl,
Life's just a joke in this vibrant swirl.

Whispers Beneath the Scarlet Veil

Underneath the scarlet sheet,
Secrets giggle, oh what a treat!
Poppies whisper to the breeze,
"Life's a party, join us please!"

A bumblebee with lots to do,
Tumbles through, quite clueless too.
"I'm on a mission!" it declares,
But poppies chuckle, twist their hairs.

Frogs leap high, with legs that creak,
While petals tease, they play hide and seek.
"We know your name, so join the fun!"
Amid the blooms, they hop and run.

Scarlet veils sway to and fro,
As laughter blooms in sunlit glow.
Underneath this playful sky,
Life's a punchline; oh, how time flies!

Petals of Resilience

Petals brave against the gales,
Stand up straight, tell funny tales.
"Life's a comedy," they sing,
"Just wait to see what joy will bring!"

Bouncing back from rain and sun,
Poppies laugh—oh, what fun!
"Did you hear that one?" they share,
As clouds drift by without a care.

Roots in soil, yet spirits high,
They wave to clouds that float on by.
"We're the clowns of the green brigade,"
With each new bloom, they're unafraid.

Through trials tough, they silly sway,
In laughter's grip, they find their way.
Against the odds, they choose to cheer,
Life's just a joke when friends are near!

Dancing in the Wake of Dawn

As morning breaks, the dew does glimmer,
Poppies twirl, growing bolder, slimmer.
"Come up and see the sun's first light!"
They prance and jig with sheer delight.

The clumsy ants, they march around,
With poppies teasing from the ground.
"Watch your step! Don't trip and fall!"
Poppies giggle, summoning all.

While shadows stretch and sunbeams splash,
Poppies bounce with joyous hash.
"Let's start the day with laughter loud,"
In the dance of blooms, none are cowed.

So shake your petals, join the throng,
In golden fields, where we belong.
With every breath, the morning sings,
Life's just a dance; oh, what fun it brings!

A Journey Beneath the Bloom

Underneath the petal's sway,
A tiny bug starts his ballet,
Twirling round on soft green grass,
Wondering if he'll ever pass.

He stumbles on the blossoms tall,
Just hoping not to make a fall.
With every prance, he seems quite grand,
Chasing raindrops, isn't life planned?

His tiny shoes get filled with dew,
A dance routine, he'll debut.
The flower chorus starts to sing,
What joy the little critters bring!

With laughter bright, the day unfolds,
In secret stories, nature holds.
Beneath the bloom, they laugh and play,
Who knew that bugs could steal the day?

Secrets of the Blossom's Heart

In the garden, whispers play,
A daisy's gossip brightens day.
"Did you hear those bees in flight?
They think they own the world, so bright!"

Roses giggle, petals wide,
"Watch them buzz, they love to glide!
But can they dress with such good taste?
We're the stars here, not a waste!"

Tulips nod in vibrant cheer,
"Let's host a ball, bring all our peers!
We'll wear our colors, shine so bold,
With stories shared and secrets told!"

Petals twirl and laughter blooms,
In secret hearts, excitement looms.
For every flower has a tale,
Of morning sun and evening gale!

The Language of Red

In a field of scarlet cheer,
A ladybug holds court so dear.
"Gather round for stories grand,
Of massive ants and wedding bands!"

With tiny wings, she takes to flight,
"Did you see that dance last night?
The roses waltzed, I swear it's true,
With daisies cheering, quite the view!"

Crimson leaves with laughter sway,
"Oh dear, what a jolly day!
Let's paint the world in shades of fun,
And dance beneath the blazing sun!"

All the blooms take part, so bold,
In joyful tales that never fold.
The language of the red parade,
Is laughter shared, and friendships made!

Echoes of Verdant Fields

On verdant fields, a breeze does tease,
Whispers float through dancing leaves.
"Did you hear that? A snail's out late!
He's strutting now, and it's first-rate!"

The daisies shout, "He thinks he's fast!
But slow and steady, won't outlast!
Let's count the bugs upon the ground,
With every giggle, joy is found!"

In emerald corners, frogs do croak,
"Here comes the sun! Let's share a joke!
What did one flower say to the bee?
'You buzz too loud; you're scaring me!'"

The echoes play in every nook,
Nature's humor, a charming book.
With every bloom, a laugh will grow,
In verdant fields, the joy will flow!

Reverie in a Blooming Meadow

In the meadow, dreams take flight,
Where daisies dance in soft sunlight.
A dandelion tries to stand tall,
But sneezes make it fall with a sprawl.

Bumblebees buzzing with clumsy grace,
Chasing pollen at a frantic pace.
They think they're skilled at the floral game,
But end up stuck, oh what a shame!

Butterflies wear a vibrant flair,
Flipping through the air without a care.
But with each flap, they seem to declare,
My landing skills? Not quite fair!

Grasshoppers jump with a silly grin,
Leaping over blooms, where to begin?
They crash, then laugh, rolling with glee,
In this meadow, joy is the key.

Heartbeats in a Flowering Field

In a field of blooms, hearts collide,
Where flowers giggle and caterpillars hide.
A tulip trips on its own bright shoe,
Laughing, it says, I'm not through!

Sunflowers stretch up for the skies,
Winking at clouds with silly sighs.
A bee whispers secrets, oh so grand,
But can't quite share; it's got sticky hands!

Petunias poke fun at the roses' plight,
"Why bloom so red? You're not that bright!"
But all is well, they laugh and sway,
In this floral scene, there's always play.

As the wind tickles each leafy face,
Flowers giggle, they're in a race.
Who can sway the most with flair?
In this flowering field, fun fills the air.

Kaleidoscope of Nature's Hues

In a world of colors, laughter rings,
Where purple meets orange, and joy always clings.
A rose tries to blush, but ends up blue,
"Oh dear," it sighs, "what's a bloom to do?"

Lilies gossip, trading petals for tales,
With tales of bees that leave silly trails.
While daisies stick out their tiny tongues,
At the soggy weeds with their muddy lungs.

A rainbow flips over every bright leaf,
Crafting giggles of delightful relief.
While clouds drift in, all white and fluffy,
Saying, "Sorry we spilled rain, it gets toughy!"

Snapdragons snap with cheeky delight,
Playing charades, oh what a sight!
With each petal's laugh, when the sun shines bright,
Nature's kaleidoscope dances in light.

Ode to the Wind-Swept Petal

A petal twirls in the gusty air,
Doing its dance, without a care.
It swirls and spins with joyful art,
But oh dear! It's lost, where's the start?

It calls to the breeze, "Let's have a chat,
I'm just a petal, and quite flat!"
The wind just laughs, with a playful tease,
"Come on, my friend, sail with ease!"

Tumbling past flowers that giggle in cheer,
The petal quips, "Do I really look queer?"
With each twist and turn, it finds its way,
In the dance of the wind, come what may.

In this frolic of nature, nothing is dull,
With petals and breezes, laughter is full.
An ode to the winds, with each happy whirl,
Life is but fun, in a petal's twirl.

Soliloquy of the Scarlet Fields

In fields so red, the blooms do sway,
They giggle softly, come what may.
With sun-kissed heads, they dance about,
"Can you believe? We're in the clout!"

They tickle bees with their laughter,
As buzzing friends chase joy thereafter.
A dandelion tried to charm,
But ended up in grass's arm.

With whispers sweet, they scheme and plot,
Jobs to distract the wandering bot.
"Let's throw a party, just for us!"
A breeze agrees, without a fuss.

Mirthful petals, nature's jest,
In scarlet attire, they look their best.
With pollen dust and carefree tunes,
Join in the fun, beneath the moons.

The Portrait of a Flower's Soul

In a garden grand, a flower dreams,
Sketching portraits with sunlit beams.
"Am I a rose or just a weed?"
It laughs aloud, "I'm in the lead!"

"Look at my colors, can't you see?
Every hue's out to outshine me!"
A tulip jests, "You're quite the bluff,
I've seen daisies made of tougher stuff."

They gossip of petals in rival hues,
Seedlings listen, caught in the clues.
"Let's paint the sky with pollen dust,
For joy in blooms is a must!"

Artistic blooms share brushes bright,
With every swish, they spread delight.
And in this light, they find their role,
Each flower's heart, a colorful goal.

Reflections in a Dune of Petals

In dunes of petals, secrets dwell,
With murmured giggles, who can tell?
A buttercup whispers, "Look at me,
I'm shining bright, we're all carefree!"

A curious wind scoffs, "Not too loud,
You'll wake the grass, and that's not allowed!"
"Let them sleep," the daisy retorts,
"We're having fun in nature's courts."

"Hey, who's the fairest in this patch?"
Grows a playful voice, so bold and brash.
The blooms just laugh, no need for pride,
In this sandy sea, they all confide.

Each petal shines in laughter's glow,
With tickling breezes that start to flow.
Together they sway, none left to rue,
In this whimsical world of vivid view.

Songs of the Chromatic Breeze

A breeze passes by, oh so carefree,
Singing tunes of blooms, oh listen, see!
"Who wants to join a flower jam?
You'll be amazed, we have the glam!"

Colors collide, like paint in the air,
"We'll dance in circles, without a care!"
The sun plays chords, the clouds hum along,
While petals sway to this floral song.

"Do you feel the rhythm?" a lilac shouts,
As laughter bursts forth from all around.
With petals spinning, like a merry wheel,
Nature's orchestra sings, "This is the deal!"

So join the fun in this fragrant spree,
Where every bloom's part of the jubilee.
With petals as voices, the world shall cheer,
For laughter in blooms is forever dear!

Interpretation of Nature's Palette

A splash of reds and yellows bright,
A dance of hues in morning light.
The grass wears green like a quirky hat,
While daisies giggle, 'Look at that!'

Bees wear stripes like they just can't choose,
While butterflies flaunt their sparkly shoes.
The sky paints rainbows on a whim,
Nature's artwork, on a playful whim.

Roses blush, too shy to boast,
While daisies say, 'We're the most!'
Nature's show is quite a sight,
A comedy in colors, pure delight.

So next time you stroll through a field so fair,
Remember the laughter hanging in the air.
For every blossom, every shade,
Is nature's joke, by humor made.

Cadence of the Colorful Blossom

Every bloom has its own jig,
Dancing sprightly, oh so big!
A daffodil spins, 'Look at me!'
While tulips sway—oh, can't you see?

In the garden, a playful tune,
Sung by petals, 'Let's dance till noon!'
The sun plays piano with gleaming rays,
While shadows waltz in the golden haze.

Giggling grass and clapping leaves,
Join the fun, a party weaves!
Nature's orchestra, loud and clear,
Budding laughter, spread the cheer!

So plant your feet on this merry ground,
And let the flowers spin around.
In joyous hues, let spirits swell,
In this silly, vibrant carousel.

Petals Beneath a Starlit Sky

Under twinkling stars we lie,
While flowers whisper their dreams nearby.
A nightingale jokes with a cheeky note,
As daisies giggle, afloat in hope.

The moon wears a crown of shimmering light,
While sleepy blooms hug the ground tight.
A sunflower yawn, 'What a day!'
'Can you believe what plants can say?'

In shadows soft, the petals sway,
Wishing on stars, they play all day.
In this floral joke, the night unfolds,
With laughter woven through the marigold.

So, snuggle close in this flower bed,
And join the laughs that blossoms spread.
For when the stars glitter in friendly jest,
Every petal knows how to laugh best.

Reverberations through the Flowering Vale

The valley hums with nature's glee,
As blossoms chime, 'Come dance with me!'
A wobbly bumblebee takes the floor,
Buzzing jokes of pollen galore.

Bright buttercups play peek-a-boo,
While violets whisper, 'What's new with you?'
Each petal chimes in a melodic spree,
Singing out loud, 'Just bee happy!'

Tulips trumpet with cheerful poise,
Sharing giggles, oh what a noise!
Laughter echoes through every flower,
Blooming joy in the sunlight's power.

So stroll through the vale where fun aligns,
With nature's chatter and sarcastic lines.
For in this place, the world's so bright,
Laughter blossoms by day and night.

Threads of Memory in Bloom

In the garden where I rest,
A poppy danced, thinking she's the best.
She twirled around with endless glee,
Claiming, "Look at me, I'm fancy-free!"

With bees all buzzing her favorite tune,
She argued loudly with the moon.
"You think you shine? Come face my bloom!"
I snickered softly, then took a zoom!

Alas, she swayed in too bright a breeze,
Her petals fluffed, she caught a sneeze.
"I'm allergic to overconfidence,"
She laughed, and danced in sheer pretence.

So here's to blooms with silly dreams,
Who twirl through life, bursting at the seams.
Even flowers can have their quirks,
In this green stage where humor works!

A Tapestry of Color and Care

In a field alive with hues so bold,
A poppy bragged, her stories told.
"I've seen the sun and snubbed the rain,"
With petals bright, she'd never complain.

Her neighbor, a daisy, rolled her eyes,
"You think you're grand? You're just a guise!
I bloom beneath the same old sky,
And yet, my style never needs to try!"

They argued long, in a flowery feud,
As a butterfly passed, in a mood.
"Can't we all bask in this splendid show?"
With winks and laughs, the garden did glow.

So here's the truth, dear friends we see,
It's fun to boast, but let it be,
A tapestry of bloom and cheer,
Is best when wrapped in laughter near!

Sunlit Reveries in Red

Under the sun, poppies lay in pose,
One popped up, striking a silly nose.
"I'm the star of this floral parade!"
While a snail creeped by, slightly delayed.

A breeze gusted by, giving her a shock,
"Hey watch it! I just styled my frock!"
She whirled and twirled, a cheeky stunt,
While daisies smirked, unbothered, they front.

The garden chuckled, a riotous spree,
As petals fluttered like confetti.
"A sunlit day's our time to shine!"
Said a wise old tulip, sipping wine.

So if you're down and life's a grind,
Just picture a poppy, not far behind.
With laughter woven through every thread,
It's the blooming spirit, not the dread!

Stems Reaching for Dreams

As I strolled through a poppy-packed field,
I could hear their laughter, so brightly revealed.
"Dreams on stems? Why, that's quite the sight!"
A ladybug giggled, in sheer delight.

"I dream of flying!" a poppy exclaimed,
"But with these roots, I feel quite contained!"
They plotted and planned with a burst of cheer,
Crafting balloons with petals sincere.

A breeze swept past, and they took flight,
"Higher we go!" they called with might.
But gravity found them, brought them down fast,
Yet all could laugh, they'd had a blast.

In a world so bright, let's all conspire,
To dream like poppies, let joy inspire.
For life's a giggle, with blooms so fine,
In this garden of dreams, let's sip the wine!

Beneath the Velvet Skies

Beneath the velvet skies so wide,
The flowers dance with silly pride.
They wave their heads, a cheerful crew,
In colors bright, a view askew.

They giggle at the clouds above,
And tease the bees with tales of love.
With every breeze, a comical sway,
In their own world, they laugh and play.

Like children running, wild and free,
They share their joy with you and me.
In fields of laughter, joy takes flight,
As poppies bask in warm sunlight.

So if you glance, just stop and stare,
You'll catch their jokes dancing in air.
A gentle nudge, a playful wink,
Life's funny blooms make us rethink.

Reflections in a Sea of Red

In a sea of red, they float and swirl,
With secrets hidden, laughter's twirl.
They gossip softly, petals aglow,
Their humor hidden, just below.

Look closely now, can you find a jest?
A flower's zinger in its quest.
With pollen whispers, giggles exchanged,
In blooms absurdly, truth is ranged.

The wind is loud, it breaks the calm,
A poppy spills its floral charm.
To tickle the daisies, steal the scene,
A comedy show, all in between.

In reflections bright, they share a laugh,
For nature's jesters, a merry staff.
In this sea of red, life's less severe,
Join in their fun, give a cheer!

The Silent Choir of Petals

In a garden grand, a choir sings,
The petals flutter, like tiny wings.
Silent notes float through the air,
With a wink and giggle, they declare.

They harmonize with bumbles near,
The bees provide the buzzing cheer.
Each blossom's humor, lush and bold,
A secret tale, in petals told.

Without a sound, they stack their jokes,
Nature's laughter, in all forms it pokes.
A silent choir, yet loud it seems,
In vibrant hues, they share their dreams.

So let them sing, those petals bright,
With laughter wrapped in pure delight.
Join the fun, let worries flee,
For humor blooms where you can see.

Threads of Nature's Tapestry

In threads of green, the poppies weave,
A tapestry that makes you believe.
With every stitch, a joke is spun,
A playful nod, a wink, a pun.

The colors clash in joyous dance,
At nature's ball, they take a chance.
With every sway, oh how they tease,
A canvas bright, they aim to please.

With petals wide, they paint the scene,
A riot of laughter, fresh and keen.
In every hue, a riddle's shared,
Each glance a giggle, lovingly dared.

In quirky threads, they hold the glee,
In nature's art, wild and free.
With laughter soft, they fill the air,
Threads of joy everywhere.

Flight of the Scarlet Wings

Flapping high in a bright parade,
Little wings dance, unafraid.
Through fields of laughter, they zoom and glide,
Chasing giggles, with joy as their guide.

Bouncing on breezes, they spin and twirl,
Wings like candy, a vibrant whirl.
In cotton candy skies, they take a dip,
Sipping sunshine on a playful trip.

With a wink and a nod, they prank the clouds,
Tickling raindrops, bringing out crowds.
They hold a contest of who can soar,
Winning hearts while the sun laughs, evermore.

And as they settle to rest on the bloom,
Dreaming of chaos in nature's grand room.
With whispers of petals, their giggles will cling,
In the silly dance of flight — joy takes wing!

Harmonies of Sunlit Blooms

In gardens where giggles freely sprout,
Flowers pipe songs, without a doubt.
With melodies sweet as honey on toast,
They form a chorus, they love to boast.

Petals in polka dots jump and bop,
Bouncing in rhythm at the flower shop.
Each note they sing, brings forth a grin,
Even the bees can't help but join in.

Dancing daisies, with ruffles so bright,
Invite the sun to join their delight.
As bees make beats, the tulips sway,
In this sunny symphony, laughter will play.

Under the sky's jovial gaze, they hum,
Mixing colors and tunes, a vibrant strum.
In the heart of nature, their joy has room,
Crafting harmony with each sunlit bloom.

Tranquility Under a Canopy of Color

Underneath the rainbow's grand embrace,
Nature's confetti plays a goofy race.
With breezes that giggle and rustle the leaves,
Colors collide in fun, as silliness weaves.

Each shade a trickster, so bold, so loud,
Tickling turtles and teasing a crowd.
In the shade where bright blossoms might pout,
You'll find them chuckling, and that's no doubt.

Whispering violets have tales to share,
While daisies reach high, without a care.
They sway with glee, in this colorful spree,
Creating a ruckus, just to be free.

So come and relax under this parade,
Where whimsy and laughter never quite fade.
In this vibrant show, there's tranquility anew,
A joyful embrace painted just for you!

Strokes of Nature's Paintbrush

With dandelion fluff and a flick of a wrist,
Nature creates a canvas, impossible to resist.
Each stroke is a giggle, each splash is a cheer,
In a gallery of fun, the artwork is clear.

Laughter spills out from the hues so bright,
Splattering joy, a whimsical sight.
Munching on colors like candy to taste,
Silly brush dances that never go to waste.

With giggling sunflowers splashed in gold,
They motivate daisies to be bold.
Creating a palette of winks and grins,
The artworks reveal where the fun begins.

So grab a paintbrush, let laughter ignite,
In the playful strokes of nature's delight.
Where colors collide and joy leaves a mark,
In every petal and leaf, there's a spark!

Melodies in the Meadow's Embrace

In fields where daisies dance and sway,
A bumblebee joins the fray.
He hums a tune, quite out of key,
While flirting with a bloom, oh me!

The butterflies wear tutus bright,
In costumes made to delight.
They twirl like dancers in the sun,
While grasshoppers cheer, 'What fun!'

A rabbit hops with style galore,
And trips on clovers, lands on the floor.
Yet giggles echo through the glade,
As nature feasts in a grand parade.

So join the laughter, join the cheer,
In meadows filled with joy and beer.
For every flower sings a song,
Where even bees can hum along!

Garden of Sighs and Sweetness

In the garden where roses pout,
The tulips tease and dance about.
They whisper jokes to bees on the run,
And laugh when snails think they can out-fun.

The daisies play peek-a-boo at dawn,
While petals play dress-up on the lawn.
A gopher tells tales of flowers tall,
While dandelions giggle at the fall.

Beetles wear hats, oh what a sight,
As fireflies turn on their lights at night.
They throw a bash, with nectar on hand,
For revelers coming from the land!

Yet hidden beneath a leafy shade,
A shy sunflower looks quite dismayed.
He wants to join the garden's spree,
But just can't find his inner bee!

Corners of Colorful Dreams

In corners where the wildflowers sway,
A sleepy tortoise thinks he can play.
He stretches slow, with dreams taking flight,
While daydreams wander into the night.

A chubby squirrel with acorns so bold,
Decides his stash is far too old.
He dresses them up in tiny hats,
And throws a party for his rat-a-tats.

The clouds above join in the glee,
As they shape shift into creatures three.
A fox, a frog, and one a bit wobbly,
Dive into laughter, quirks, and fun gobbly.

Yet through it all the rabbits decree,
"Join us dear, let your spirit be free!"
They set the scene, with daisies in tow,
For a garden party, just so you know!

Vibrations of a Floral Heart

In the blossoms where giggles bloom,
A sunflower flaunts its lush costume.
It sways to the beat of the buzzing tunes,
While grass shimmies under glowing moons.

A daisy tells tales with petals spread,
Of secret galas where dreams are fed.
While busy ants pull a conga line,
To impress the ladybugs, oh how divine!

The lilacs conduct with flair and zeal,
As the whole patch joins in for a reel.
Where blooms compare their growth in height,
While laughing clouds drift into the night.

So gather 'round, join in this spark,
In this floral rave from dawn till dark.
For every petal and leaf in sight,
Plays a part in this joy tonight!

Emotions Untouched by Time

In fields where laughter sprinkles light,
A flower sneezes, takes to flight.
It tickles bees, they buzz around,
While worms in dirt just laugh, unbound.

Time slips on like a silly song,
While petals wink and sing along.
Each bloom a jest, a fragrant quirk,
Nature's humor laughs at work.

Under the sun, they dance and prance,
A floral twist in nature's dance.
With every gust, they toss their heads,
Making fun of all the beds.

So here we stand, with heartbeats light,
With blooming giggles, oh, what a sight!
In petals soft, our worries fade,
As time forgets, and jokes cascade.

Serenity in a Cloud of Color

A breeze so soft, it starts a riddle,
As flowers laugh and gently twiddle.
A red one whispers, 'What's up, blue?'
'I'm here to stomp and dance with you!'

The daisies chuckle, rolling around,
As butterflies, in laughter, abound.
Their painted wings, a comical sight,
Tickle the air, then take to flight.

'Oh dear,' says yellow, 'where's my hat?'
As poppies giggle at all of that.
With colors bright, the world seems odd,
In this cheerful chaos, we take a nod.

So skip along this joyous spree,
In shades of humor, wild and free.
With every bloom, a laugh to share,
In nature's jest, we find our flair.

Vibrance in Nature's Silence

Amidst the silence, blooms collide,
A burst of giggles, nowhere to hide.
Roses arguing, 'I'm the best,'
While daisies debate on who's more blessed.

In vibrant hues, they paint the day,
With laughter bright, they come out to play.
A bee stumbles, tipsy on cheer,
And flowers chuckle, 'Here comes our beer!'

Sunshine giggles at shadows near,
As petals mold into jokes we hear.
The wind whispers, 'You bloom, I swoon,'
A riot of color, a silly tune.

In every rustle, a punchline shared,
Each colorful bloom, completely unprepared.
In this garden of glee, we skip and rhyme,
In nature's laughter, we dance with time.

A Tapestry of Blossoms and Time

Once upon a stem, the violets jive,
While dandelions plot how to thrive.
'Blow me away,' they cheerfully shout,
As winds collect laughter, casting doubt.

A minty scent hangs thick in the air,
As flowers whisper, 'Life is fair!'
With petals twirling, they start to weave,
A tapestry of giggles, who could believe?

The sun drops hints, a tickling tease,
A tapestry made of colors and bees.
And every bloom, with a wink and a grin,
Pulls you into the laughter within.

As seasons turn, and flowers sway,
Catch the chuckles in this bouquet.
With every blossom, a punchline fine,
In time's embrace, let joy entwine.

The Fragility of Floral Dreams

In a garden of giggles and dreams,
Petals prance in whimsical beams.
A bumblebee trips on a high-flying whim,
As daisies debate on their fashion limb.

Winds tickle stems, making them sway,
While tulips gossip about the bouquet.
'Why so serious?' a hydrangea teases,
'Let's throw a party, invite the breezes!'

Buds burst forth with a gleeful cheer,
But the sun whispers, 'I'm not quite here!'
Cloaked in shadows, the flowers frown,
As the moon brings laughs from the sky's gown.

In this land where blooms all jest,
The fragile dreams never need a rest.
With laughter dancing on each bright leaf,
Nature's humor brings delightful relief.

Remnants of a Blooming Memory

Once a bloom with stories to share,
Now just a ghost in the gardener's lair.
'Remember when I twirled in the breeze?'
Asking weeds for old tales, with such ease.

Their roots entwined, they chuckle and sigh,
'Oh remember that rush from the bees flying high?'
And the cat with a penchant for chasing the flies,
Once wore a crown made of petals, oh my!

Sunshine chuckles at shadows so bold,
As daisies recall how they once were gold.
But petals grow weary, and memories fade,
Turning to compost, the stories cascade.

Yet in laughter and whispers, they linger near,
Remnants of joy that draw us to cheer.
In the garden of laughter, where blooms once spun,
Life holds its memories, oh, isn't it fun?

Illuminations in the Meadow

In a meadow alive with chaotic flair,
Colors collide in a vibrant affair.
Buttercups giggle as daisies dance,
Foxgloves flirt, giving life a chance.

The sun plays peek-a-boo with tall grass,
While crickets prepare for their evening sass.
Each petal's secret whispered without care,
'What's the latest gossip? Oh, do we dare?'

Clouds overlap like bases of a game,
As wildflowers yell out each other's name.
'I'm the star in this broad daylight!'
The poppy claims, with a wink that feels right.

With laughter echoing under the sky,
Every bloom seems to wink, oh my!
In this meadow of mayhem, so bright and jolly,
Nature's humor sweeps over, a carefree folly.

Ties of the Wildflower's Song

Among the hues where wildflowers play,
They sing a tune in a breezy ballet.
Lilies twirl with a wiggling charm,
While violets giggle, their bases in yarn.

Each bloom arrives with a colorful tale,
Of love and of laughter, they never curtail.
'Have you heard the joke about the rose?'
'What? It's stuck in a vase, I suppose!'

In the meadow, chaos weaves a bright tune,
As petals debate the best time for June.
Together they dance, in silly delight,
Under the gaze of the stars shining bright.

So here's to the laughter that flowers promote,
With roots intertwined, they joyfully gloat.
In the symphony of colors, they sing all day,
The ties of their song simply bloom and play.

The Dance of Spring's Heart

In a meadow where giggles bloom,
Flowers sway, dispelling gloom,
Petals twirl like dancing clowns,
Tickled by their silliness crowns.

Bees are buzzing, oh so sly,
While butterflies float up high,
Grass tickles toes of passing feet,
Nature's laugh, a joyful treat.

Clouds wear hats of cotton white,
Sunbeams play hide and seek with light,
Raindrops join a splashy game,
Spring's heart dances without shame.

So let us join the wild ballet,
In this merry dance, we'll play,
With every step, a giggle shared,
In this springtime, love declared.

Brushstrokes Beneath the Dappled Sun

In fields where colors laugh and sing,
Dandelions wear crowns of spring,
Crickets chirp their silly tunes,
While bees hum along with cartoons.

Sun casts shadows, fun shapes arise,
The trees wear coats of green surprise,
Squirrels prance in a furry race,
Nature's art, a playful space.

With paintbrushes of golden rays,
They splash the world in fun-filled ways,
Colorful chaos, a vibrant spree,
Life is a canvas, wild and free.

So grab a brush, come join the fun,
Beneath the light of the dappled sun,
Make each moment bright and bold,
In this gallery, we unfold.

Garden of Forgotten Dreams

In a garden where lost dreams hide,
Giggling flowers can't abide,
Chasing fireflies in the night,
They twinkle with sheer delight.

Weeds wear hats made of wishes past,
While laughter echoes, unsurpassed,
Vines twist tales of silly dreams,
In this laughter, sunshine beams.

The moon winks at the sleepy scene,
With every shade of playful green,
Charming the night with its soft glow,
Where even shadows dance and flow.

So wander here, forget your woes,
In this garden where kindness grows,
Let every laugh and every cheer,
Cultivate joy, year after year.

Fleeting Moments in Bloom

In a hurry, flowers rush to show,
Roses contemplating 'what's this glow?'
Tulips giggle, all in a row,
As daisies whisper, 'A little slow!'

The sun peeks through in a mischief way,
Tickling petals, come out to play,
Butterflies laugh as they flit about,
In this dance, there's no room for doubt.

Moments flutter, oh so fast,
Holding on to laughter that can't last,
Each bloom chuckles, 'Let's have some fun!'
In this fleeting dance, we're never done.

So seize this laughter, this joyous light,
In moments of bloom, take flight,
For life's a joke, a cheerful sigh,
Catch these giggles before they fly.

www.ingramcontent.com/pod-product-compliance
Ingram Content Group UK Ltd.
Pitfield, Milton Keynes, MK11 3LW, UK
UKHW020609180125

4163UKWH00039B/174